D1087877

Yellow Animals

by Teddy Borth

ABDO
ANIMAL COLORS
Kids

abdopublishing.com

Published by Abdo Kids, a division of ABDO, PO Box 398166, Minneapolis, Minnesota 55439.

Copyright © 2015 by Abdo Consulting Group, Inc. International copyrights reserved in all countries. No part of this book may be reproduced in any form without written permission from the publisher.

Printed in the United States of America, North Mankato, Minnesota.

102014

012015

 THIS BOOK CONTAINS RECYCLED MATERIALS

Photo Credits: iStock, Shutterstock

Production Contributors: Teddy Borth, Jennie Forsberg, Grace Hansen

Design Contributors: Laura Rask, Dorothy Toth

Library of Congress Control Number: 2014943707

Cataloging-in-Publication Data

Borth, Teddy.

 Yellow animals / Teddy Borth.

   p. cm. -- (Animal colors)

ISBN 978-1-62970-699-3 (lib. bdg.)

Includes index.

1. Animals--Juvenile literature.   I. Title.

590--dc23

                    2014943707

Table of Contents

Yellow

Yellow is a **primary color**.
Yellow cannot be made
by mixing other colors.

Mixing Colors

⬤ **+** ⬤ **=** ⬤

⬤ **+** ⬤ **=** ⬤

⬤ **+** ⬤ **=** ⬤

⬤ **+** ⬤ **+** ⬤ **=** ⬤

Primary Colors

⬤ **Red**

⬤ **Yellow**

⬤ **Blue**

Secondary Colors

⬤ **Orange**

⬤ **Green**

⬤ **Purple**

5

Yellow on Land

Flower crab spiders **hunt** on flowers. Their yellow color helps them hide. Other animals cannot easily see them.

6

The citrus bearded dragon is yellow. It is a popular pet. It can change color when it fights.

9

The golden dart frog is small.
It is one of the most **poisonous**
animals. Its poison can kill
an elephant!

Yellow in Air

The comet moth is on the money of **Madagascar**. Adult moths cannot eat. They only live for 5 days.

American goldfinches shed
their feathers twice a year.
Males are bright in the spring.
They are dull in the winter.

Dragonflies come in
many colors. Yellow is
just one of those colors.

17

Yellow in Water

Brain coral looks like a brain.

It can live for 900 years!

It can grow 6 feet (2 m) tall.

Yellow boxfish are bright

when they are young.

Their color fades with age.

21

More Facts

- Insects and birds are drawn to the color yellow.

- **Poisonous** animals use yellow as a warning. Attackers avoid bright yellow animals because they know of the danger.

- Yellow is the color of wealth (gold), sunshine, happiness, and wisdom.

Glossary

hunt – to follow and attack something.

Madagascar – the island country off the coast of southeast Africa.

poisonous – causing sickness or death.

primary color – a color that cannot be made by the mixing of other colors.

secondary color – a color resulting from mixing two primary colors.

shed – to lose fur, feathers, or skin and grow it new.

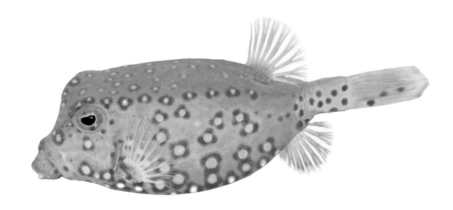

Index

abdokids.com

Use this code to log on to abdokids.com and access crafts, games, videos, and more!

Abdo Kids Code:
AYK6993